Quest for Quivira

QUEST for QUIVIRA

SPANISH EXPLORERS
ON THE GREAT PLAINS
1540-1821

Thomas E. Chávez

Dedicated to my daughters
Nicolasa Marie and Christel Angelica

Library of Congress Number 91-067395

IBSN 1-877856-05-3

Edited by
Ron Foreman and
Greg McNamee

Designed by
Kimura/Bingham Design, Tucson, Arizona

Printed by
Arizona Lithographers, Tucson, Arizona

Cover:
Detail of Segesser II, a painting on buffalo hide
depicting the ambush of the Pedro de Villasur
expedition in Eastern Nebraska on August 13, 1720.
Fray Juan Mirquez rushes to administer last rites to
wounded Spanish troops. He is led by Joseph Naranjo,
a Santa Clara Pueblo Indian. They are under attack by
Pawnee and Oto Indians, and French soldiers. From
the collection of the Palace of the Governors, Museum
of New Mexico, Santa Fe.

Printed on recycled paper

CONTENTS

AN OCEAN OF GRASS

In 1821 William Becknell crossed the Great Plains with five partners and some pack animals laden with goods. He was welcomed in Mexico's northern department of New Mexico "with apparent pleasure and joy." Mexico had just become an independent country with open borders. He quickly exchanged his merchandise for specie (coins), gold, and silver. Word of his good fortune spread throughout the eastern settlements of the United States, and the Santa Fe Trail began its fascinating march through history.

Becknell's route became a corridor of commerce between the western United States and northern Mexico for the next sixty years. Silver from Chihuahua and material goods from the Mississippi River Valley incited a flurry of merchants to load wagons and mules and venture across the plains. Through the years travel journals, newspapers, novels and, finally, histories told the story of the Santa Fe Trail.

Becknell and his colleagues were not the first to travel the Great Plains—at one time labeled the great American desert. But until the end of the nineteenth century Europeans did not even attempt to settle in the area. How could a descendant from Europe survive without trees, their source of fuel and material for shelter?

Water travel was the most efficient mode of travel until the inception of the railroad. Although there are rivers in the plains—all tributaries of the Mississippi—water was not abundant enough to provide for convenient travel by boat or ship. The eventual route of the Santa Fe Trail was landlocked. Only the eastern terminus of the trail, which was not in the plains, provided water transportation.

Significantly, the first Englishmen and Frenchmen to penetrate the plains did so on rivers. Even the fur trade, made popular by romantic notions of mountain men, primarily depended on transporting supplies and furs across the northern plains as far as they could get on the Missouri River. Thomas Jefferson sent out Meriwether Lewis and William Clark in part because the United States held a slim hope that a "northwest passage," a water route through the continent, might be discovered. This is the same idea that originated with Christopher Columbus's sailing west to try to reach the oriental trade; instead he bumped into a land mass. Until the early part of the nineteenth century a water passage was still sought through this great impediment.

Europeans and their descendants in the Americas believed in this water passage for almost three centuries. The Spanish called it the Straits of Anian. They inherited Columbus's dream to go west to the Orient. Eventually United States President James K. Polk would fight a war to achieve that end, although the water passage was no longer a part of the scenario. In the middle of the continent a huge inhospitable barrier that had become a great desert in American minds impeded the way.

Spaniards, too, found the plains less enticing for habitation than other areas. But they did not have the same foreboding about them as did other Europeans. One reason might be that they encountered this vast interior stretch of land fairly quickly after they arrived in the New World. Like other Europeans they usually settled along the sea coasts and navigable rivers. Mexico City—which had been discovered as Tenochtitlan, the capital city of the Aztec empire—was an exception. Mexico City benefited from trade carried on in both the Atlantic and Pacific oceans. Its central inland location with reasonably quick access set up the city as an administrative focal point for the transfer of Spain's oriental trade, which helped it become rich.

The other exception to the pattern of settling close to water transportation was the colonization of New Mexico in 1598, with its capital village of Santa Fe, founded in 1610. Unlike Mexico City and vicinity, New Mexico really had no function as a lucrative trade center. In fact, early Spanish administrations considered abandoning the colony because it was of no real benefit and it cost the Crown money. Nonetheless, New Mexico survived. The colony existed not on the Spanish frontier, the edge of European civilization, but as an island in the wilderness. Throughout the Spanish colonial period until Mexican independence and the subsequent opening of the Santa Fe Trail, New Mexico existed as a pocket of Spanish society distant from the people of its birth by thousands of miles.

To understand why Spaniards would live in landlocked New Mexico, it is best to begin with Columbus who, irrespective of his place of birth, typified most of the Spaniards who sailed the world over in the next couple of decades after his 1492 voyage. The route of his first trip took him first to the Canary Islands off the west African coast, which were possessions of Spain. From those islands he began the grand adventure that would change world history.

During his trip Columbus routinely and almost stoically recorded each day's distance. It is no wonder that his crew suggested that they should navigate in directions toward where they thought there might be an island or two. He reasoned that they had come too far to deviate from their course; they had better move ahead in fulfillment of their mission. The crew accepted the rationale. We can only imagine what went through the minds of those people as day after day passed without sighting land.

The attitude exhibited by those sailors is the same attitude with which Spaniards quickly penetrated into the interior of this "tierra incognita." Within fifty years of Columbus's first trip, sons of Spain had fanned out all over Central America, into South America, to the present-day Southwest of the United States and onto the Great Plains, over what would become the Santa Fe Trail.

The first Spanish expeditions into the area of New Mexico began with rumors of an indigenous population living in cities and towns to the north like those of central Mexico. Europeans, especially Spaniards, found such populations more attractive than nomadic people. Fulfilling the Catholic church's mandate to bring new souls into the fold was much easier with sedentary rather than migratory people. Sedentary populations accumulated more wealth, as the Aztecs and Incas demonstrated. Could there be another Tenochtitlan, another Mexico? Or, more simply put, if the Spaniards found such civilizations in the central and southern parts of the New World, then there must be another in the northern region.

As a result, Spain initiated a number of expeditions. Two of those forays traveled onto the plains; one of them, on its return, traversed a majority of what would become the Santa Fe Trail. That journey, known as the Coronado Expedition, originated in Mexico and launched from the city of Compostela northwest of Mexico City. The goal was to find Quivira, those civilized and rich peoples of the north.

Vásquez de Coronado and his men would travel into the unknown looking for the specific in a general area, suffering uncertainty and hardship.

And the journals and logs kept on these overland expeditions are strikingly similar to those of the many sea voyages of exploration. Instead of traveling to the Canary Islands, this initial expedition searched for what would become the Canary Islands of the plains. With the Pueblo Indians centered in the Rio Grande Valley in what would become New Mexico, Spain found its island, situated on the western edge of the plains.

The plains were vast, flat, and, to the minds of the time, uninhabitable. Because they were covered with the tall grass that constantly swayed in the breezes, more than one early chronicler compared them to an ocean. Pockets of trees along river bottoms with drinkable water were the islands of the plains. Those islands might be inhabited by Indians. The best way to travel the plains was from island to island. All the future routes followed that pattern, which was initiated by the Indians before the Europeans came. From their first knowledge of this area the Spanish wanted to explore this grand land to see what islands existed and what might be gained with contact on the other side.

Eventually the plains came to be the area separating the westward expansion of northern Europeans, primarily Englishmen, and southern Europeans, primarily Spaniards. New Mexico was a Spanish island on the western edge of the plains. The eastern edge of the plains, like a seacoast, became inhabited, first by the French and then the English and their political descendants.

New Mexico was not only the jumping-off place for plains travel from the west. It was geographically located to become the focal point for the eventual meeting of the approaching frontiers moving from the east and south. The Santa Fe Trail, the modern story of which began with the independence of Mexico, was the umbilical cord that would forever turn the Hispanic population's attention to the United States and away from any ruling body in the south. ❧

VÁSQUEZ DE CORONADO

In the summer of 1540, Vásquez de Coronado's captain Hernando de Alvarado first heard of the plains at a Pueblo Indian village near present-day Bernalillo, New Mexico. Vásquez de Coronado had moved into the region with an army of around 350 Spaniards and a thousand friendly Indians. An Indian leader from Cicuye, now known as Pecos Pueblo, and an Indian from the plains living at the same pueblo talked to Vásquez de Coronado about civilizations of the plains. The Pecos Indian called Bigotes denied the existence of riches. Another, called El Turco (the Turk), claimed to know better.

The Turk was sent with Alvarado. They went first to Pecos, which at the time was the largest pueblo in the area. Today a National Historical Park on the Santa Fe Trail, it is situated on the Pecos River with access to and from the plains. Its people had long been influenced by their proximity to the plains. Pecos had hosted trade fairs where Plains Indians came in to trade with the Pueblos. The Pecos people were careful not to let the Plains Indians into the village but made them set up camp outside the pueblo. The pueblo itself had been constructed on a rise above the river and was built in two separate clusters of buildings with a wall around the entire village.

From Pecos Alvarado traveled northeast to the Canadian River and then followed it for approximately 260 miles, which would have placed him in the Texas Panhandle. He never saw the "large settlements in the farther part of that country" that the Turk talked about. For the moment he had spent as much time as he was allowed so he returned.

Undaunted, Vásquez de Coronado set out for the plains in late April of 1541. He took a southerly route down the Pecos River. Again following the advice of the Turk, the army left the river and traveled far south of the Santa Fe Trail into central Texas before deciding to turn north. There they stopped listening to the Turk, who they realized was trying to get them lost.

The Turk miscalculated the Spaniards' ability to deal with vast spaces. He must have known that these strangers had some concept of where they were. Not only could they calculate sunrise and sunset, or observe the stars, but one poor person was assigned the task of counting his steps so they could calculate distance! The unfortunate Turk did lead them away from his native land, but the truth was learned from other Indians, and the expedition headed north using other and more truthful guides. At this point, the main body of the army was sent back to the Rio Grande Valley. They had been traveling through the vastness for thirty-seven days, covering a distance of about fifteen miles a day for a total of approximately 550 miles. (Columbus encountered land on the thirty-seventh day of his voyage.) When Vásquez de Coronado revealed his decision to send the majority of his army back so he could travel quicker and lighter, those asked to return "declared that they all wanted to die with him and did not want to go back."

Unlike confinement to a ship at sea, Vásquez de Coronado's men could wander off from the main body of the army. The expedition's chronicler, Pedro de Castañeda, wrote that many fellows became disoriented, some of them missing for two or three days at a time:

Wandering about the country as if they were crazy, in one direction or another, not knowing how to get back where they started from. ...Every night they took account of who was missing, fired guns and blew trumpets and beat drums and built great fires, but yet some of them went off so far and wandered about so much that all this did not give them any help, although it helped others. The only way was to go back where they had killed an animal and start from there in one direction and another. ...It is worth noting that the country there is so level that at midday, after one has wandered about in one direction and another in pursuit of game, the only thing to do is to stay near the game quietly until sunset, so as to see where it goes down and even then, they have to be men who are practiced at it.

An anonymous member of the expedition wrote that travel on the plains was so dangerous that "it is [as] if one was traveling on the sea."

After another forty-eight days of traveling, Vásquez de Coronado reached some villages on the Arkansas River near the present town of Lyons, Kansas. He called the place Quivira. He had reached an island that did not contain the great civilization he had hoped to find. Nonetheless, after such a long and incredible journey, rather than immediately return, he used Quivira as a base of operations for further exploration dispatching a number of small detachments in all directions. Vásquez de Coronado's men penetrated into the areas as far east and north as the present states of Missouri and Nebraska.

Castañeda described the land as flat all the way to Quivira, where he began to see some variety in the topography. The men found Quivira to be similar to Spain. They were told of a great river a little farther on and later found out that it was the same one discovered by Hernando de Soto that same year. The river then named Espiritu Santo, or Holy Spirit, later came to be called the Mississippi. Many of the fruits and plants in Quivira were familiar to the Spaniards. They found large quantities of flax but noted that the Indians "do not know how to use it."

Satisfied that no more could be done in Quivira or beyond, the small group of thirty returned by a more direct route, traveling an estimated 530 miles. They were led by Indian guides knowledgeable about the plains and who used the sun to gauge a direction and then shot arrows in that direction as they traveled. The return journey followed most of the route of the Santa Fe Trail. These men had actually anticipated the trail to New Mexico. And this was accomplished in 1541!

The abundance of buffalo, which the Spaniards referred to as cows, amazed the explorers. During the return trip, the main part of the army relied on the buffalo almost exclusively as their source of food—which caused some digestive problems. The "cows" continually impressed the explorers. One of Vásquez de Coronado's soldiers anonymously reported that they were "the most monstrous thing in the way of animals which have ever been seen." And there were so many that one soldier did "not know what to compare them with, except with the fish in the sea."

As far as the Spaniards were concerned, the plains were uninhabited. The Indians they encountered followed the cows, hunting them and tanning the hides, which they took to settlements bordering the plains, "each company going to those [settlements] which are nearest, some to the settlements of Cicuye [in New Mexico] and others toward Quivira." They grouped these plains people into two types who called themselves Querechos and Teyas. Both groups of Indians were well-built, painted, and enemies to each other. They impressed the Spaniards as being better warriors and having superior figures than either the Pueblo or Quivira Indians. They traveled "like Arabs," using dogs to transport their baggage on Moorish-like "pack saddles with girths." The Indians did not remain on the plains for the winter but left for the settlements.

Castañeda found the plains people to be a "kind people and not cruel. They are faithful friends." Perhaps this last assessment grew out of the help the expedition received from the Indians. Nor did the chroniclers overlook the many ways these Indians used the buffalo. They tanned the hides to trade, make clothing, and cover their dwellings. They dried the meat to transport it more conveniently. The explorers also noted that the Indians drank the blood of the cows.

The Spaniards found the plains awesome. They recorded the country as "spacious and level" and, as noted, dangerous to the inattentive. They especially noted the flatness. Castañeda wrote that after traversing over five hundred miles of land, they did not see another mountain range apart from the one they had left in Tiguex [New Mexico],

nor a hill nor a hillock which was three times as high as a man. Several lakes were found at intervals, they were round as plates, a stone's throw or more across, some fresh and some salt. The grass grows tall near these lakes, away from them it is very short, a span or less. The country is like a bowl, so that when a man sits down, the horizon surrounds him all around at the distance of a musket shot. There are no groves of trees except at the rivers, which flow at the bottom of some ravines where trees grow so thick that they were not noticed until one was right on the edge of them.

Yet none of these people seemed overawed by what they had seen. God, so they wrote, had chosen them to see all that they had seen and he had left for others to search beyond Quivira and, perhaps, to locate the fabled cities and Straits of Anian to the north. Vásquez de Coronado had planned a return to Quivira and had ordered his men to prepare for the trip after the winter season. However, a near-fatal fall from his horse sealed God's will, and the general ordered the army to return to New Spain.

Only the Franciscan friars and their helpers received permission to remain. Fray Juan de Padilla became the first person to travel up the eventual trail when he, an African, a Portuguese servant named Andres do Campo, and a handful of Indians returned to Quivira. Fray Padilla achieved martyrdom when the Indians at Quivira killed him because he tried to go and minister to their enemies. Campo survived to tell the story, retracing his steps across the plains along the future Santa Fe Trail when he made his escape. ❧

NEW MEXICO,
THE LANDLOCKED COLONY

When Vásquez de Coronado and his army returned to New Spain, the General gave testimony and filed reports in Mexico City. Nonetheless, interest in the far north waned, for that island of Indian villages beyond the northern deserts was too poor. No riches had been found. No evidence of a northwest passage had been discovered. Only some impoverished sedentary Indians and a vast expanse of land had been encountered.

Besides, attention quickly became diverted south when silver was discovered in north-central New Spain in the area of Zacatecas in 1546. This discovery gave rise to a whole new episode in Spanish colonial history, for the silver lode existed beyond the realm of what had been the Aztec empire. This was the land of the nomadic and unconquered Chichimeca Indians. The resulting movement of Spanish colonial society into the mining areas led to a vicious war that lasted over four decades and ended only when the Spanish used Indians to conquer Indians, settling Indian allies from central Mexico among the Chichimecas.

Eventually more wealth would be taken out of the earth in this area, later known as Nueva Vizcaya, than was ever taken from the Indians. This original rush, a harbinger of what would happen when gold was discovered in California in the nineteenth century, became the first American frontier movement.

Not coincidentally with the end of the Chichimeca wars and the establishment of Spanish society in Nueva Vizcaya area did the Franciscan priests start talking of New Mexico—the first time it was called by that name. Had not some of their brethren been left there many years before? The Indians were sedentary and should be converted. Moreover, the land had not been thoroughly explored. What of the waterway to the north? In 1581,

*"Shaggy cow," the buffalo as pictured by Francisco López de Gómora
in his* Historia *in 1554.*

permission was given for a missionary reconnaissance. Fray Agustin Rodriguez, with two other priests, nine soldiers led by the elderly Captain Francisco Sanchez Chamuscado, and sixteen to twenty Indians journeyed up the Río Grande into New Mexico. They explored west to the pueblos of Acoma and Zuni and then turned east to the Galisteo villages. At San Marcos Pueblo, which they called Malpartida, they inquired about the cows on the plains and were told that they were only two days' march from the cows. The Pueblo Indians even volunteered the information that the buffalo herds occasionally came within twenty-one miles of the pueblo. After securing some guides, the small group headed off to the plains. They traveled through the Pecos region out onto the plains and turned northeast until they reached a branch of the Canadian River, which they followed. At one point they went forty hours without water, but continued nonetheless.

They, too, found the buffalo fascinating, good eating, and easy to hunt. There were so many of the animals that the expedition traveled for miles through them, and they "are so large that when seen in the midst of a plain they resemble ships at sea or carts on land." Seeing these new shaggy cows was one of the reasons for going onto the plains. They more than satisfied their curiosity in the Canadian River Valley. After a couple of weeks they returned from Cibola, "the Plains of the Cattle," as they called the area.

The Rodríquez-Chumuscado expedition returned to New Spain without either of its leaders. All the priests had been left in New Mexico, and the old captain died on the way back. The arrival of the survivors in Mexico in April 1582 stimulated more interest in the north. Seven months later Fray Antonio de Beltrán and Antonio de Espejo led an expedition to New Mexico with the goal of rescuing the friars left behind earlier in the year. They quickly learned that the priests had been killed. The party then split up. Beltrán and some of the men left for home. Espejo and the majority explored some more before returning south by following the Pecos River. While the river took them out onto the plains, they never gave thought to traveling northeast toward Quivira.

Official interest in settling this island to the north began to grow. The motives had little to do with these first expeditions, aside from the fact that Spain now knew that the area could be inhabited and thus become a base for further exploration and, if need be, defense. There was the crux, for Francis Drake, sailing under the rival flag of England, had made a number of surprise appearances on the west coast of the Americas. He had raided Spanish ports in Chile, Peru, and Mexico. He refurbished his ship, the Golden Hind, at a northern California bay. Rumor spread that he had discovered a transcontinental strait, the elusive northwest passage. Could that discovery be the reason for his sudden appearance on the Pacific seaboard?

Spain needed to counter this British challenge. New Mexico was a perfectly situated locale from which further exploration in search of the water passage could be launched. At the very least, British shipping could be harassed. Whether this was the prevailing argument for the decision to permit the settlement of New Mexico or not is subject to conjecture. At least this reason was one of the motives along with the more obvious and rational arguments for conversion being forwarded by the Franciscan friars.

The decision to settle New Mexico gave rise to a grand competition among various would-be governors to receive royal permission to lead the expedition to instill Spanish civilization in the faraway land. Before the legal expedition of Juan de Oñate in 1598, a couple of unauthorized expeditions left for New Mexico. Apparently, the leaders of these bootleg journeys were trying to take a page out of Hernán Cortés's book and avoid prosecution through the success of their actions. However, both expeditions fell short of Cortés's exploits.

The second of these two unauthorized expeditions is of some interest. In 1593 Francisco Leyva de Bonilla and Antonio Gutiérrez de Humaña led an expedition that was blatantly illegal. Their act demonstrated Spanish infatuation with the myth that another wealthy civilization would be found in the north and, in the process, left just enough information about its activities to tantalize our imaginations. Only a Mexican Indian servant survived to tell the sordid story of Leyva's and Gutiérrez's exploits.

After spending a year based at San Ildefonso Pueblo and exploring in New Mexico they headed out beyond Pecos Pueblo and the "Vaquero Indians" to explore the plains. Although we have no tangible evidence, it appears from the testimony of the Mexican Indian, Jusepe Gutiérrez, and some evidence gathered from a subsequent expedition led by Juan de Oñate's sergeant-major Vicente de Zaldívar, that they followed Vásquez de Coronado's old return route along the Santa Fe Trail. After crossing two rivers and traveling fifteen days, they came upon a settlement of Indians so large it took them two days to travel through it. The Indians lived in houses, jacals built of poles and covered with straw. They had planted fields of corn, squash, and beans. This was probably Quivira, in the area of Wichita, Kansas, although some historians believe that the site of this great village was near the junction of the Arkansas and Walnut rivers in southern Kansas.

The expedition proceeded in a northerly direction for at least three days when Gutiérrez stabbed and killed Leyva, who had been leading the group. Gutiérrez took over the expedition. At this point, some of the Indian servants fled. Only Jusepe made it back to New Mexico. He arrived in New Mexico in 1598 after Juan de Oñate and his officially sanctioned settlement had moved into the area with 129 soldiers and their families, eighty-three wagons, and some seven thousand head of livestock.

Jusepe's account inflamed the desire of the leadership of New Mexico's first legal settlement to see the great Quivira of earlier expeditions. The trip would not be so hard anymore, in that Oñate had moved a permanent base of operations to New Mexico. Oñate wasted no time following up on Jusepe's story. He assigned Vicente de Zaldívar the task of leading the expedition onto the plains using Jusepe as a guide. Because of Jusepe's presence, this expedition was the best prepared to have ventured there. The guide's loyalty was firm and his knowledge was firsthand for he had lived with various tribes that traveled on the plains. He had been a captive of at least two, and possibly three, tribes for more than four years. Zaldívar instructed Jusepe to retrace the route of the previous expedition, and the guide dutifully followed his instructions.

Zaldívar's party of about sixty soldiers set out in the fall of 1598. They found two of Leyva's and Gutiérrez's campsites. How far Gutiérrez and his followers traveled before they were killed in a prairie fire set by the Indians—as Zaldívar found out later—is unknown. Quite possibly, they went up what became known as the Pawnee Trail, a north-south route through Kansas. If so, they may have traveled up the Santa Fe Trail and turned left on the Pawnee Trail, possibly making it as far as Nebraska. This may have been the second expedition out of New Mexico to do so.

Like previous travelers, Zaldívar's men were impressed with the buffalo that "have beards like billy-goats" and decided to take some of the animals back in captivity. A stockade was erected and some buffalo directed into the trap, whereupon the Spaniards learned that herding buffalo was a little different than their previous experiences with four-legged animals, for Gaspar Pérez de Villagrá, one of Oñate's captains relates that "they began to stampede, rushing about like a raging whirlpool, raising an immense cloud. Had our soldiers not been stationed on an eminence they would no doubt have been trampled to death beneath the hooves of these savage beasts." With the stockade in shambles and the men thankful for their lives, no further attempts were made to herd buffalo. Could this have been the first roundup in the West?

Three years later Vicente de Zaldívar and most of his men, including Jusepe, retraced their steps. This time they were being led by Juan de Oñate himself as part of a larger expedition. Oñate took the exploration of the plains seriously. Otherwise, why go himself and why invest so much in this expedition's equipment? If crediting Zaldívar as the first cowboy is tentative, then Oñate's 1601 expedition's fame for making history is not. Along with seventy to ninety men, some Indian servants and some seven hundred animals, Oñate took eight wagons (sometimes translated as carts), six drawn by mules and two by oxen. These "carts" were not the locally made, two-wheeled carretas that Frederick Remington depicted in some of his nineteenth-century drawings of the Santa Fe Trail. These were commercially made, four-wheeled wagons brought to New Mexico from New Spain. Later customized versions of these wagons would be called "prairie schooners" and used by travelers from the United States.

Some historians would later claim that Oñate's trip did not amount to much because it did not travel any farther than earlier expeditions. Still, it was the largest to penetrate as far as the others. Oñate achieved his goal of reaching Quivira. He did not go beyond this now-familiar locale. None of the previous expeditions, however, had taken along wagons and artillery.

Another interesting tidbit has been overlooked. Oñate's group seemed to enjoy the plains. They did not find them foreboding and, in fact, exclaimed about their lushness, good land, abundant game, and water. Even suffering a thunderstorm seems to have been a minor inconvenience. They spent five months on the trail from the day they left New Mexico on June 23 until the return to their town of San Gabriel on November 24. Yet, even with hardships, the journey's chronicler dutifully noted that travel from the point of origin at San Gabriel, just north of today's Española, to Galisteo took four days. Then they moved on to the Pecos River in five days. Another day was spent getting to the Gallina River, after which they traveled three more days to get to the Canadian River. They followed this last river west across the Texas Panhandle. Here, apparently for the first time, they called the plains "Cibola," the same word they used for buffalo. As they traveled deeper into the plains, they "came to some deep ravines and gorges but, as for hills, we found none whatever, as the land over which the carts had to travel was level and easy to cross." As with any ocean, the Spaniards found the flatness of the plains an advantage rather than an obstacle to travel. Nor did they feel threatened by Plains Indians, even when they came upon a tribe of five thousand people who lived in hide and branch dwellings or when they arrived at Quivira, a town of twelve hundred houses. There seemed to be no sense of danger in the record of the expedition.

They came upon friendly Apache, Kansa, or Osage Indians that they called Escanjaques. They obviously encountered the Wichita Indians, who were the Quiviras. The Escanjaques became irritated when Oñate and his men would not allow them to sack an abandoned Wichita village, and they fought a pitched battle receiving many wounds.

The chronicler also mentions a chief named Catarax who told Oñate's

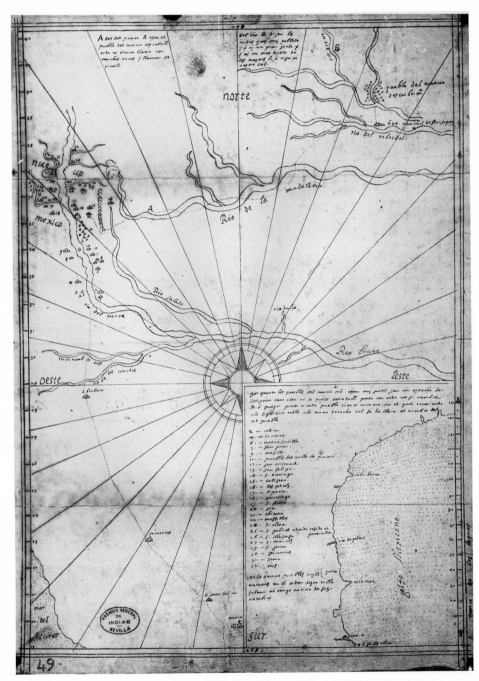

Map of New Mexico, c. 1602, showing the route Oñate took onto the plains.
Original in the Archivo General de Indias, Seville, Spain.

group of other Indian towns and villages. His name resembles the word Tatarax, which means "chief" among the Wichita. Vásquez de Coronado and those of his expedition who wrote of their experiences used this last word for chief when writing about the same Indians. The similarity of the two words as used by expeditions sixty years apart helps identify the Quiviras as Wichitas as well as place the two expeditions among the same Indians.

Recognizing that their mission had been fulfilled, Oñate and his officers agreed that they should return and file reports to the king about "the high quality of the land, the many people, the wealth in cattle [buffalo]...and the good places with the necessary materials for establishing important settlements." They found Kansas appealing.

The return trip from Quivira to San Gabriel took fifty-nine days, a number that anticipates later crossings. With this trip, the Spaniards accumulated enough knowledge to compile a map with Oñate's route. Drawn in New Mexico by Enrico Martinez in 1602, the map accurately shows where Quivira was in relation to New Mexico. It also shows that the plains of the Santa Fe Trail were no longer mysterious, for they had been charted.

The settlement of New Mexico heralded a new epoch for the Indians of New Mexico and all those surrounding the territory. Plains Indians recognized a new factor in their lives. The Quivira Indians sensed this change when Oñate's men successfully defended themselves against the Escajaques, who were enemies of the Quiviran people. As a result, six hundred Quivira Indians traveled to New Mexico to solicit Spanish friendship, trade, and protection, "so that they would help them fight against their enemies." Then they noted that "the Spaniards had traveled a great deal out of their way on the route they took and if they had gone directly north, they would have arrived quickly." Fray Zarate Salmerón wrote in 1626, almost twenty years later, that "according to what they [the Quivira Indians] said, one should go by way of Taos and through the lands of the great Captain Quima, across those plains." Oñate had taken his army and wagons along the general route of the Santa Fe Trail, going south to the Pecos River and avoiding the mountains before heading northeast to the Canadian River. But by following the Canadian River as long as he did, he for the most part traveled south of what would become the actual route. The Quivira Indians knew a more direct route, which according to Salmerón, would amount to what would become the actual trail, including the Taos cutoff. ❧

SEVENTEENTH-CENTURY EXPEDITIONS

Myths of new kingdoms and the Straits of Anian persisted. The kingdom of Tidam, bordered by the kingdoms of Chiullescas, Guismanes, and Aburcos, was supposed to be somewhere toward Quivira. Somehow word of the new Christian religion had spread in this kingdom. One priest argued that more exploration was needed to learn "through what medium and methods Our Lord has manifested [Catholicism] to them." "The truth is," he added, "that in not carrying out fully the exploration of this land, His Majesty loses a great world."

Oñate was eventually replaced as governor of New Mexico by Pedro de Peralta, who brought with him instructions that if he should discover the Straits of Anian he should find the best port possible and defend it from all foreign intrusion. Interest in the far north did not wane in Mexico City. Nor did interest in converting the Indians of Quivira. Apparently because the priests in New Mexico had more than enough Indians in the Rio Grande Valley and vicinity, there were not enough clerics to send to Quivira.

According to the Franciscans, Plains Indians started requesting priests to go live among them. The friars told the story of a woman dressed in blue who visited the Indians and "used to tell them, each in his own language, to come without delay and summon the priests that they might teach and baptize them." They further described her as "young and beautiful." Fray Alonso de Benavides, the former father custodian, head priest in New Mexico, identified this mysterious lady as Madre María de Jesús, commonly known as María de Agreda, a sequestered nun in Spain who claimed she could preach to the Indians in and around New Mexico through bilocation.

Probably as a result of the Lady in Blue and the enthusiasm of New Mexico's priests, the infusion of thirty friars made the mission to Quivira feasible. Two priests traveled out onto the plains, where, according to

María de Jesús de Agreda, "The Lady in Blue." Copperplate engraving from
Tanto que se Sacó de Una Carta *of Fray Alonso de Benavides in 1631.*

Benavides, ten thousand Indians met them before they reached Quivira. The priests continued on to that "kingdom," for they had received word that the Lady in Blue had been in Quivira recently.

This missionary effort may have been the same effort that another friar, Father Estevan de Perea, wrote about. He wrote of an expedition in which he, two other priests, twenty soldiers and the Governor, Francisco de Sylva, traveled into the country north of the route to Quivira following the advice of that early contingent of Quiviran Indians.

For most of the seventeenth century the record of plains travel is unclear. Evidence does exist that New Mexicans continued to move onto the plains. Fray Benavides, who left New Mexico in 1629, wrote of Quivira with such knowledge that there can be no doubt of the garnering of information from further unknown trips. He wrote that Quivira and its neighboring kingdom of Aixaos were well known for their "greatness and wealth." He further stated with some exaggeration that "we know from evidence and personal inspection that there is in this kingdom...a very large quantity of gold. Every day we see Indians from there who trade with ours and who testify to this fact." He continued that the best strategy was to settle the area so the King of Spain would benefit from the area's wealth.

Perhaps more telling than Benavides' attempts to build up the religious cause through his thinly veiled use of tales of gold is his detailed suggestion on how the area of Quivira should be settled and supplied. He noted that to travel inland to Quivira requires overland trips of great distances. But Quivira's proximity to the Gulf of Mexico and a bay he calls Espiritu Santo, apparently the place where he believed the Mississippi River emptied into the Gulf of Mexico, located somewhere between the present towns of Galveston and Corpus Christi, suggests that the crown might cheaply benefit from the trade of buffalo "hide and wool." Furthermore, the friar accurately noted that the closest line to the sea from Quivira was to the Gulf of Mexico and that it was a much shorter and more peaceful alternate route over which the king would save "large sums on escorts of soldiers and on wagons." Such a plan would effectively bring into the imperial system the rich port of Havana, thereby creating a system of commerce throughout the far north and the Carribean. Other information hints at the extensive travel that was going on and, by then, being taken for granted.

Interestingly enough, one of New Mexico's true scoundrels in the seventeenth century left one of those hints. Diego Dionisio de Peñalosa's corrupt regime as governor of New Mexico (1661-1664) resulted in a trial before the Inquisition in Mexico City before he was expelled from the Spanish empire. He spent the rest of his life trying to convince Britain and then King Louis XIV of France that they should set up a colony on the Gulf coast of Texas or Louisiana. He argued that it could be used as a base of operations to move into "Gran Quivira" with its riches and from there to New Mexico, thus seizing the northern part of Spain's New World empire. To bolster his arguments, Peñalosa produced the journal of a grand expedition that he supposedly led to Quivira; eventually, a map was compiled in France based on his information. Except for the myth of gold and silver, his information was fairly accurate and even revealed a bit of additional information about the plains between New Mexico and Quivira. Although he lied about the expedition, for he never went onto the plains, the journal apparently was based on a true expedition.

Possibly he borrowed from the experience of a little-known, amazing, journey led by Alonso Baca, who according to Peñalosa left Santa Fe in 1634 with "some soldiers." Baca apparently traveled along the Santa Fe Trail route. He is reported to have advanced almost to a big river that one historian claims is the Mississippi. Indian hostilities forced him to return. Baca and his men did visit Quivira, a fact that gives direction to his journey. Recurrent problems between the Spanish settlers and Pueblo Indians resulted in another series of events that hint of further New Mexican activity to the northeast. In the early 1660s, a group of Pueblo Indians from Taos and Picurís left their respective pueblos to flee the Spaniards. They moved out on to the plains and placed themselves into servitude to the Apaches. While on the plains they built a series of small-roomed structures resembling pueblo architecture near the present border of Colorado and Kansas. Along with their Apache masters they opened up trade with Quivira. No doubt they also traded with Pueblos in New Mexico, thus establishing their new settlement as a conduit for commerce.

Soon after the New Mexican authorities learned of the exodus of the northern Pueblo Indians, they reacted by sending an expedition out to bring them back. Sometime around 1665 Juan de Archuleta was dispatched to find the Pueblo Indians. With twenty soldiers and some Indian guides he located them and noted their dwelling places, calling the place "small rooms," El Cuartelejo. The authorities claimed that he brought back all of the Pueblo Indians. This is probably not true, for the settlement at El Cuartelejo lasted until 1727, over a half a century.

By the 1670s the Pueblo Indians began to show signs of resisting Spanish impositions. For good reason, sporadic resistance and subsequent complaints sprang up. This culminated in 1680 when the Pueblos unified and violently expelled the Spanish from the northern Río Grande Valley. From the exiled Spaniards' point of view, this problem superseded everything. No expeditions left for Quivira until after the New Mexicans, now living in the El Paso area, returned to New Mexico in 1693. The resettlement of New Mexico began a new epoch for New Mexican history as well as the history of what would become the Santa Fe Trail.

By the time of the Pueblo Revolt, every river and Indian tribe had been located and named in documents and maps. Even on the far side of the vastness, names like the Río Rojo, the Río San Lorenzo, and the Río de Jesús María had been given to rivers that would later receive the less imaginative names of North Platte, South Platte, and the Platte itself. Not one Indian tribe of the period was omitted. Cuartelejos, Jicarillas, Flechas de Palo, Calchufines, Palomas, and other Apache groups were known and recorded. The Wichitas, Utes, Pawnees, and Kansa Indians all had been contacted. Some Plains Indians had even become allies to the newcomers, and some lived among the Pueblo Indians.

Upon their return to New Mexico, the Spaniards had three problems to solve. First, they needed to reestablish relations with the Pueblo Indians, who were no longer mystified by these people. While some of the natives welcomed the Spaniards' return, others were not so sure. As a result, Diego de Vargas, the new governor and captain-general of New Mexico, met resistance and had to retake Santa Fe as well as conduct a subsequent campaign against resistant pueblos.

The second problem had to do with reestablishing alliances with nearby non-Pueblo Indians. These included Apaches, especially the Humanos. As Spaniards soon learned, some of the Plains Indians, too, had pressing reasons for accepting Spanish overtures. A new group of Indians, called Comanches, had moved south from their original home with the Shoshone in southern Wyoming. The Comanche Indians had inserted themselves between New Mexico and Quivira.

The French posed a third problem. King Louis XIV approved the plans of Robert Cavelier, Sieur de La Salle, who had traveled the length of the Mississippi River and wanted to set up a French settlement at the river's mouth. La Salle traveled beyond the Mississippi and was left without a usable ship on the Texas coast at Matagorda Bay in 1684. His 180-man expedition ended up marooned in Spanish territory. Possibly after attempting to reach Quivira or New Mexico, and then the Mississippi River, the colony mutinied, killed La Salle and eventually dwindled to only a half dozen survivors, one of whom ended up in New Mexico. This was Jean l'Archevêque, who became a Spanish citizen and traveled up to New Mexico with Diego de Vargas in 1693, just four years after he had been rescued in Texas by Spaniards.

Spanish reaction to the French threat was quick. A number of sea expeditions sailed along the Gulf coast, apparently trying to find the Bay of Espiritu Santo. In the process of searching for La Salle, the Spanish charted the coast. By 1690, just six years after La Salle landed, the Spanish had established two missions in Texas near the Neches River, and a year later Texas became an official frontier province.

The change in attitude affected New Mexico as well as the importance of the plains. As with Texas, New Mexico became a defensive outpost.❧

VIOLENT ENCOUNTERS
AND RUMORS OF FRENCHMEN

Settlement and exploration became tools to protect the empire. Quivira and the other villages or societies, real or not, had to be defended. Foreign interests could not be allowed to usurp Spanish territory. There could be no doubt of French presence or of a threat from these European rivals. If Vargas had any doubt, he only had to look in his own ranks to see l'Archevêque.

All three problems facing the new governor were interlocked. As Vargas learned, the French were nearer than expected. By 1700, they had permeated the Illinois country, moved into the Mississippi Valley and up the Missouri River, and had begun to move out onto the plains. French influence disrupted Plains Indian relationships and made Spanish alliances with these Indians nearly impossible. While subduing the Pueblo Indians, Vargas acquired firsthand information on the complexity of the problem, for he constantly heard stories of the French from Indians who had heard about these other white people while trading with Plains Indians.

In October 1696 Vargas found Picurís Pueblo abandoned and learned that the inhabitants had fled to the plains. He immediately set out in pursuit. From the beginning, this journey, which probably did not leave the present confines of New Mexico, proved to be an arduous trip. Vargas noted that the trail of the Taos and Picurís Indians he was following was difficult because of inclement weather. At one point, rain completely obliterated the trail. On the other hand, Vargas surmised that the "severe cold" would necessitate nighttime fires for the renegades to keep warm, so he dispatched scouts at night to try to locate the Indians.

Four days into the pursuit, Vargas and his men reached the plains. There they found evidence of the enemy who had scattered so fast they left the ground strewn with tent poles. Vargas ordered a quick pursuit which ended when, "we reached an open region without any trail at all."

They soon encountered some of the Indians. After some fighting and the capture of one unnamed Indian leader, whom the Picurís claimed was the source of all their problems, a victory was claimed.

The next day the army, now burdened with its booty, moved out into a country that Vargas described on various occasions as open with ravines, chaparrals, rocks, and trees. But the expedition came to a halt because of another characteristic of the plains to which Vargas and company became the first non-Indian witnesses but, fortunately, not the victims. Vargas tells the story best:

On the twenty-eighth of the month of October... because of a heavy snow and windstorm in a strange country, (I) gave orders that the army should halt. Ten other persons of the rebels, for whom I also ordered supplies, had drifted in the night before. Pushing on till about two in the afternoon, I was forced to rest on account of the heavy snow. Thus being closed in by the darkness of the storm, I missed the place to which we were journeying. I remained with the army to spend the night without water on the plain.

We can only imagine the details of travelers who were caught in blizzards on the plains and lived to tell the story. What is interesting is Vargas's matter-of-fact and brief telling of the tale. Nevertheless, this first reported encounter with winter weather on the plains was severe.

Vargas left the majority of his men and the captive Indians in camp, and rushed back to civilization for aid. On November 7, Vargas arrived at Pecos Pueblo with some of the officers of the army. He reported,

From here I sent relief to the army which I left. I had been on the march since the twenty-eighth day up to this day in the fury of snowstorms and driving blizzards which obliged me to stay two days, unable to move from the spot. I, as well as all the people, ran great risk in going on foot because the snow was so deep, the cold and winds, moreover, making a storm. Every day dawned upon many dead horses. Others, benumbed and frozen, were almost gone. Even in the short distance of four or five leagues, when the count was taken, we had lost more than two hundred horses and five mules belonging to the soldiers and to me.

Vargas had heard stories of Frenchmen brought into New Mexico by Indians. The year before his expedition he heard tales of "white and blond" men helping Indians war on their neighbors. In 1696, before his expedition, a tale of white men preparing to attack Quivira had been reported by Apaches visiting Taos. These stories were used by the governer to justify a request for more artillery to improve Santa Fe's fortifications against the French. Whether Vargas's request was a serious reaction to actual Apache reports or he was reporting apocryphal tales to justify his request will never be known. But French presence across the plains, at the other end of the Santa Fe Trail, was considered close enough to New Mexico to get the attention of Vargas as well as Spanish officialdom in Mexico City.

Perhaps demonstrating how commonplace plains travel had become, the subsequent reports matter-of-factly relate how the Navajos, who lived northwest of the Spanish settlements, had become accustomed to the long trip to Quivira. Nevertheless, in 1694 the Navajos claimed that they had fought the Pawnees, who the Spanish called Pananas, and their French allies on more than one occasion. At a trade fair of that same year the Navajos had among their spoils some Pawnee children whom they hoped to ransom to the Spanish for a good price. When they were turned down, the children were beheaded by the Navajos. The account of this atrocity so offended the King of Spain that he ordered the use of royal funds to prevent the recurrence of such an event.

Juan de Ulibarrí, who had been with Vargas in 1696, received the assignment to lead the next expedition to Cuartelejo in 1706. Governor Francisco Cuerbo y Valdes had received a message that some of the expatriate Indians sought to return from the plains if they would be guaranteed favorable treatment. In early July, Ulibarrí enlisted twenty presidial soldiers, twelve settlers, and one hundred Indians from various pueblos for this rescue mission. Santa Clara Indian Joseph Naranjo captained the Indian auxiliaries. The son of Domingo Naranjo, a Pueblo leader in the 1680 rebellion, Joseph had sworn allegiance to Vargas and now was considered captain of all Indian auxiliaries in New Mexico. He became a legend in his own day.

The expatriate Frenchman l'Archevêque also went on this expedition. Expectations of encountering some evidence of French intrusion may have precipitated his participation. On the other hand, all able-bodied men in New Mexico were expected to serve in its defense, so this expedition may have been his turn along with the eleven other settlers who were included.

Rather than going directly to the plains via Pecos, they chose to go north following the steps of Vargas and, perhaps, the advice of the Quivira Indians of the previous century. More likely, the above reasons plus the excitement at Picurís Pueblo over the return of their kinsmen justified the northern route, for the Picurís Indians supplied the expedition with quantities of cotton and woolen blankets as well as extra horses for their kinsmen to use on the return journey.

In Taos, a pending attack of Ute and Comanche Indians delayed the expedition. Then, on the east side of the mountains around Cimarron, they encountered a succession of friendly Indians, including the Jicarilla Apaches, who agreed with the warning that the expedition was in danger of Apache groups. The commander himself reported that a guide "advised us that we would undergo much suffering because there was no water and, if any, very little and that far ahead, and that the trail was only open land." Ulibarrí faithfully noted the foreboding advice and continued with his journey. He bought off potentially hostile Apaches with gifts of knives, tobacco, pinole, and corn biscuits. In contrast to Oñate's expedition a little more than a century earlier, this one had trouble staying on course and finding water.

The expedition traveled from Cimarron to the vicinity of the present-day site of Trinidad, Colorado. In the process, Ulibarrí did something different in plains travel or, at least, something heretofore unrecorded. Ulibarrí ordered that all the expedition's tired horses be left in the care of the Jicarilla Apaches until the Spanish returned from Cuartelejo. This was a show of extraordinary confidence and trust in the Jicarillas and in his ability to succeed in his mission in spite of the dire warnings.

From the Trinidad area the expedition traveled directly north for forty leagues to the Arkansas River or, as Ulibarrí noted, "We...arrived on the great river which all the tribes call the Napestle," a name that New Mexicans used into the nineteenth century. In the area of Pueblo, Colorado, on July 30, the expedition turned east, leaving the mountains and moving directly onto the plains. Almost immediately the expedition was in trouble. The buffalo trails soon disappeared and the men had to depend on more clever techniques to direct them. Ulibarrí observed that the Indian guide, "took his direction from hummocks of grass placed a short direction apart on the trail by the Apaches, who lose even themselves here. In this way they had marked out our course." The commander adds, "All of this was of no use to us for, although the Indian took especial care, we became lost entirely."

Finally, after finding water by luck, Ulibarrí decided to send scouts out to locate more water before moving the expedition. The scouts ran into some people from Cuartelejo who helped guide them. They were greeted at Cuartelejo by Apaches and Pueblos alike, who assisted the Spaniards in locating the Pueblo Indians wishing to return to New Mexico.

While waiting for everyone to be gathered, the Cuartelejo Apaches asked Ulibarrí if he would join them in a raid upon the French and Pawnees. The New Mexican commander seemed impressed with their sincerity in the matter, but he did not want to be caught on the plains when the first snows came. He had personally experienced the unpleasantness of blizzards on the plains with Vargas ten years earlier. He resolved the problem without alienating the Apaches by giving the leader a rifle and promising to join them in a subsequent expedition.

He did hear more about the French. He was told the story of how the Pawnees, accompanied by some French, had set out to attack Cuartelejo at a time when the Apaches were out hunting buffalo. The Pueblo Indians at Cuartelejo were warned and were able to abandon the area, thus leaving no human booty for the Pawnees. The Cuartelejo Apaches returned just as the Pawnees, becoming suspicious, had decided not to move into the abandoned villages but to retreat. Apache scouts sent out to watch the retreat caught up with a white man and a white woman whom they killed. The white man was bald, so they scalped the woman and returned with her hair. The Apaches even volunteered the information that the woman was pregnant! They also brought back a red-lined cap, a kettle, a large gun, and some powder found with the man. In addition, the Spanish found three other French weapons among the Cuartelejo Apaches. The French, unlike the Spanish, had no qualms about giving or trading firearms to the Indians. Although he tried, Ulibarrí could not get a fix on where the French were located.

The expedition began its return trip on August 11 with sixty-two Pueblo Indian returnees. Others, although no count is given, chose to remain in Cuartelejo. They followed the same route back, reaching the Arkansas River on August 17 and the Jicarilla camps on August 27, where they received all the animals left in their care. Four days later they arrived at Picurís Pueblo, where all the returnees were released to a joyful reunion.

This journey was a success. Some Pueblo people were brought back, an alliance was in the making with the Cuartelejo Apaches, a new part of the plains to the north had been traversed and, thanks to Ulibarrí's journal, information on Indian groups migrating into the area had been gathered. Ulibarrí gave the best description of Cuartelejo in the known documents, noting that the Pueblo people lived in more than one village, even listing some of the village names. He observed that the Indians were cultivating crops, among which were maize, watermelons, pumpkins, wheat, and kidney beans. He also recorded the names of the various Apache tribes he had met or heard about. The plains had become a place of dynamic change as the ebb and flow of pressure among different tribes washed across the vastness.

MOUNTED ENEMIES

Ulibarrí had gone north of the present trail after Trinidad. With his route the Spanish had covered all the area northeast toward Kansas and Missouri.

With Ulibarrí's expedition also came a subtle change in the Spanish mentality toward plains travel. A generation of men now embarked on a series of expeditions that would carry on through the eighteenth, and into the early nineteenth century. For the most part, these new travelers were born in the New World and had never been on the high seas; their descriptions of the plains have fewer references to the ocean. The conquistadores gave way to traders and soldiers respectively making money and defending the homeland. The romantic, and probably rusty, metal armor of the early travelers gave way to leather jackets and bullhide shields called *adarqas.* Ulibarrí personified this new breed.

Through the early years of the eighteenth century, Indian hostilities had built up. The Pueblo Indians, as well as Spanish settlers, were subject to increasing attacks from Plains Indians. Navajos ended a long peaceful relationship to begin raiding closer to home in the Río Grande Valley. Their raids necessitated a number of punitive expeditions to the northwest into Navajo land, which diverted the Spaniards' attention from the northeast.

The expeditions that did go east did not venture far onto the plains. At least none are recorded as doing so. The Faraones were the main problem close to the east and the campaigns against them seemed to accomplish little in the way of curbing their raiding.

In 1712, Governor Juan Ignacio Flores Mogollon led a futile campaign against the Faraone Apaches. Less than two years after Mogollon's effort another expedition was so ineffective that the Faraones immediately raided both Picurís and Taos pueblos. Then they raided Picurís Pueblo again while the governor was holding a war council to decide what to do about them.

The decision of the governor's council to actively seek out and punish the culprits foretold the motive of the next two expeditions to the northeast. They would be punitive expeditions, rather then expeditions of exploration. Combined with a third expedition, the forays to the northeast were defensive strategies with no attempt at setting up trade. The third expedition left as a reconnaissance mission to find a French army.

The audacity of the Faraones needed to be dealt with immediately and the leaders of Picurís and Taos pueblos could not have agreed more. In fact, the Picurís Indians had managed to overtake the second Faraone raiding party and retrieve all their stolen horses. And here is a hint of another factor causing immense changes.

Although none of the travel journals state that the Navajos, Faraones, or any of the other Indians circling New Mexico had become mounted, it is a safe assumption. The Faraones were stealing horses and mules and, like all the other Indians groups involved with New Mexico, had long since learned that such animals were of far greater value as a mode of transportation than as a source of food. The use of horses would explain the great distances traveled regularly by the Navajos and the rapidity with which stories of Pawnee and French depredations traveled to New Mexico. The horse, coupled with the French contribution of the firearm from the other side of the plains, caused a movement of Indian groups and disruption of plains relationships. The Pueblos had become mounted by the eighteenth century. The fact that the Faraones and, subsequently, the Comanches and Utes proved to be fairly adept at avoiding the punitive expeditions might indicate that they, too, had become mounted and thus were not easy prey like their predecessors. The fact that these Indians were mounted might also explain why the New Mexican expeditions had to take precautionary measures like night marches and, at times, even seemed loath to make contact. A Spaniard knew the tactical advantage the horse provided.

In reaction to the Faraone affront, in 1714 Juan Paez Hurtado was assigned to organize an expedition to seek out and punish them. There could not have been a more hardened veteran of campaigns in New Mexico than Paez Hurtado. He had served with Vargas, been an interim governor of New Mexico, and participated in numerous campaigns. As a veteran of earlier expeditions against unmounted enemies who had not been on any recent expeditions, he became frustrated.

The expedition traveled a fairly great distance over already traversed territory. With a large force of forty presidial soldiers, twenty settlers including l'Archevêque and 151 Indian allies from nine different pueblos, the expedition embarked from Picurís Pueblo, crossed the mountains, and traveled through the Mora Valley which they described as having "an abundance of pastures and meadows to refresh the horseherd." The trail here was easy with "evergreen oakwood, poplar, and pine trees." Beyond the Mora Valley the army traveled to the Canadian River, then called the Río Colorado. They continued on the old route following the Canadian River into the Texas Panhandle where the expedition turned around somewhere north of the present city of Amarillo, Texas.

They never encountered the Faraone Apaches and this resulted in an unusual act of frustration by Paez Hurtado. As he reported, the army came to a lush spot where he had been led to believe they would find an enemy *ranchería*. Instead they found no evidence of an encampment. Paez Hurtado called his chief scout before him. Although no name is given, this person presumably was Joseph Naranjo. The commander questioned the scout about the lack of success and when the scout had no answer, according to Paez Hurtado, he had him lashed fifty times. In the context of the previous campaigns and Paez Hurtado's experience, this punishment was unusual. No earlier report of an expedition records such treatment for auxiliary scouts, especially one, if it was Naranjo, who had such an exemplary record in the service of Spain.

The Ute and Comanche Indians quickly replaced the Faraone Apaches as the next prime threat to New Mexico from the plains. These two tribes had requested an armistice with the Spaniards in 1704 but their raiding during the Ulibarrí expedition as well as forays against some of the pueblos, ended what chance there was for peace. The Jicarilla Apaches now petitioned for protection against these new hostile people from the plains. A council of war held by Governor Antonio Valverde y Cosio advised that punishment should be meted out to the recalcitrant tribes.

Valverde also received pressure from the viceroy in Mexico City who was worried about French intrusion on the plains. Then in 1719, Spain and France declared war upon each other. The viceroy was concerned that all the stories and rumors from New Mexico might indicate a potential French invasion from the north. Valverde organized an expedition against the Comanches and Utes that could double as a reconnaissance mission, perhaps picking up information about the French, thus satisfying the viceroy's concern.

By the time Valverde, who was leading his own expedition, had gathered his army, he had over 600 Indians from the pueblos as well as Jicarillas. Sixty presidial troops and forty-five settlers filled out the expedition that had over 850 horses, a drove of sheep, casks of wine, and one keg of very good brandy especially for the governor. This was the largest expedition to leave for the plains since Vásquez de Coronado's army 178 years earlier.

Again employing the invaluable experience of Joseph Naranjo, the army used Taos as the place of embarkation on September 20. Within four days they crossed the mountains and reached the by-now very familiar Canadian River. However, Valverde chose not to follow Paez Hurtado's footsteps. Maybe Naranjo advised the Governor to try a different route—that of Ulibarrí. The army moved north over the same mountainous ridge and onto the plains near Trinidad, Colorado. They traveled by a river that later became known as the Huérfano and, as the expedition journal reads, "on the road, (one) of the many which go to and from Santa Fe and its settlements." His route is almost, if not exactly, that over which caravans of trade goods would rumble to and from the United States and Mexico little more than a century later.

While continuing "on the road" and "leaving a high sierra on the west with much level ground stretching toward the east," some of the men also contracted poison ivy. The affected were in great discomfort, especially those on whom the malady spread to the genital area. Fortunately, one person accidentally found a remedy for the sickness while chewing on a longtime delicacy of the New World—chocolate. No longer able to stand the swelling and itching, he spread the salivated chocolate on his face and, no doubt to his surprise, found instant relief. Word of this discovery spread throughout the ranks and soon everyone was relieved.

On October 6, the army reached the Arkansas River somewhere east of Pueblo, Colorado, where they followed the river eastward for ninety miles and met some Cuartelejo Apaches. As before, the Cuartelejos were anxious for the Spaniards to help them against their enemies. In anticipation of the arrival of the Spaniards, all the people of Cuartelejo were moving down to the Arkansas River to meet them. In spite of the willingness of the Cuartelejo and Carlana Apaches to help fight their mutual enemies, Valverde apparently felt that a buffalo hunt was more pressing than pursuing the enemy. Valverde even joined the hunt, running down and spearing a cow.

After satisfying his hunting appetite, the governor set out to meet the main contingent of Cuartelejos, but came upon another herd of buffalo and a hunt ensued. Four days later, the expedition had not moved beyond the spot of the second hunt.

Although the journal is not clear on this point, the size and inactivity of the expedition began to pose problems. Valverde wrote that eating buffalo meat and "gruel made from corn meal," which was becoming scarce, necessitated dispatching one of his officers and some men to return to Taos for more provisions.

By now it was late October and the expedition had been out long enough and late enough in the season that Valverde figured the people back home might become concerned. Among the messages sent back to New Mexico was a letter for his lieutenant governor, Pedro de Villasur, who had been left in charge. In the letter, the governor gave his assistant the impression that he was already marching on his return to Santa Fe. Perhaps the governor was foreseeing the length of time it would take for the letter to reach Santa Fe.

On October 21, over one thousand Apaches pitched camp with about two hundred tepees on the opposite side of the river from the New Mexican expedition. From this point on, all thought of Comanche and Ute Indians ceased, for the Cuartelejos (now also called Palomas) had many tales about the French. The French were moving into the region just beyond Cuartelejo and had allied with the Pawnee and Humano Indians. That the Humanos suddenly appeared east of Cuartelejo casts some doubt on the total veracity of what was being said. To prove their point, the Cuartelejos noted that one of their chiefs had received a gunshot wound. Valverde had the man brought before him. The governor asked who gave him his abdominal wound? The man answered that the French, Pawnees, and Humanos attacked him and his village while they were harvesting corn. Others added that the French had built villages, two of which were larger than Taos, on the banks of the Mississippi River. Furthermore, the French had given some "long guns" to the Indians and had taught them how to use them. The French "also carried some small guns suspended from their belts" and called the Spaniards derogatory names. As a result, the Cuartelejos continued, new Apache tribes had been moving into the area and away from the French and Pawnees.

The closeness of the winter season and this new information about Spain's European rival dictated that Valverde return to New Mexico. The fact that French weapons were spreading throughout the plains could not be refuted or ignored. Even if the French didn't actually have an army on the plains, the prospect of firearms in the hands of plains peoples was frightening. The governor pieced together a fairly accurate picture of what was happening on the other side of the plains. Actually, in 1719, Charles Claude du Tisne had visited the Osage Indians in Missouri and eastern Kansas. He gave them a gift of guns and traveled on to the southern Pawnees. There he again left guns, received a mule with a Spanish brand, and was refused passage through their lands to the Comanches. The Pawnees would not allow him to establish contact with their enemy. Claude du Tisne reported that there was a Pawnee barrier that had to be overcome before there would be an open road to New Mexico.

In late November, Governor Valverde wrote to his viceroy. Everything, he scrolled, that he heard from the Indians agreed with what he had been told by Joseph Naranjo. In summation, he said, the French appeared to have a strategy "to penetrate little by little into the land," which was easy to do over "this country." He then added,

I am prepared ... to attend to the matter personally, or my lieutenant general will do so, that is, the making of a reconnaissance of the enemy in order to report to your Excellency in regard to everything the most certain knowledge, if in the interior I have no new superior order.

Meanwhile the governor would keep a vigilant lookout for the French, beginning with the reconnaissance expedition he proposed. The viceroy agreed.

By the middle of June the following year, the reconnaissance party, led by his lieutenant governor Pedro de Villasur rode out of Santa Fe. Joseph Naranjo and Jean l'Archevêque, once again, were included among the forty-three soldiers and three settlers. By now, both men were well traveled and experienced on the plains. In fact, the governor's dependence on Naranjo for information about the French and the scout's familiarity with the route of this expedition indicates that he had already been to the Pawnee villages on the Platte River in present-day Nebraska. Apparently Naranjo had gone there on an unchronicled journey. Naranjo himself claimed to have been to the Platte River and to Cuartelejo on four different occasions. All the officers and most, if not all, of the men had been to Cuartelejo, at the least.

The expedition followed the common practice of going to Taos to organize and pick up Pueblo Indian auxiliaries before crossing the mountains and heading on to the country of the Pawnees "to make a reconnaissance of the settlements which they say those of the French nation have established." Nor were they under any illusion about the country over which they would travel. One soldier described the familiar territory as a "passable land, a hard plain, with very much grass or hay and considerable streams." Probably based on what he heard from Naranjo, the governor wrote of the country of the Pawnees in a letter to the viceroy,

Their Plain is so extensive that all agree it embraces not less than one hundred and fifty leagues [about 300 miles] more or less, and there is not on the whole of it anything more than some briar bushes and a few poplars along the rivers and small streams which cross and water it.

The expedition crossed the mountains from Taos and traveled through Jicarilla territory to the Canadian River. Then they headed northeast skirting the mountains by Raton and continued to Cuartelejo where, once again, the Indians welcomed the Spaniards. From Cuartelejo they traveled east into Kansas where they encountered the Pawnee trail. Following the trail north they came to the Platte River in what is now Nebraska. The force pushed on, traveling down the Platte River to the confluence of the Loup River where on Friday, August 9, they set up camp.

Naranjo and his scouts picked up the trail of a large Indian group and began to follow the tracks. Before long they located a large Pawnee camp and tried to make contact. When they heard that a white man was with the Pawnees, l'Archevêque wrote a letter in French in an attempt to open a dialogue. All this was to no avail and, sensing a hostile attitude in the Pawnee camp, the force withdrew to the earlier camp site at the Loup and Platte rivers. A fairly restless night was spent in camp as the men heard strange sounds, including barking dogs.

On Tuesday morning, August 13, just as the New Mexicans were breaking camp, a volley opened up an engagement that, in some respects, resembled the battle at Little Big Horn. The attackers did not have horses, so they waited until the proper moment to make sure their foe did not have a mounted advantage. The initial volley apparently stampeded the horses, diverting the mounted horse guard who needed to round up the animals.

Of the forty-six Spaniards on the expedition, thirteen survived the ambush. In addition twelve of the sixty Pueblo Indian allies died. The latter included the intrepid Joseph Naranjo. Apparently, the overwhelming number of enemy Indians attacking the New Mexicans met stiff resistance, for they had enough damage inflicted upon them to let the survivors quit the field without pursuit. The Cuartelejo Apaches helped the survivors to Cuartelejo where they were allowed to recuperate before continuing on to Santa Fe.

Importantly, the Villasur expedition points out an aspect of the history of the Santa Fe Trail that is frequently overlooked. There were different reasons for traveling over the plains and, in the process of those many trips, history was being made. Sometimes the noteworthy event was not the trip at all but something that happened as a result of, or on the trip. In Villasur's case both the journey and the event of the ambush are important. His party covered great distances from Santa Fe, New Mexico, to eastern Nebraska in a relatively short time—especially on the return. The idea that Indians with French weapons would ambush a Spanish contingent with Pueblo Indian allies in the center of the North American continent as early as 1720 is astounding.

The tragedy of Villasur's group led to an investigation of the whole northern frontier, including New Mexico. Governor Valverde, long since replaced by his nephew Juan Domingo de Bustamante, was forced to pay a minor fine for placing an inexperienced Villasur in charge of the expedition. The bigger question had to do with the Plains Indians. ❧

THE COMANCHE THREAT

The Comanches quickly became the most feared of all plains people. Their prowess and aggressiveness pushed other tribes out of their homelands. Many sought alliances with the people in New Mexico to help defend against these adept plains warriors.

The Jicarillas were desperate for Spanish protection against the Comanche onslaught. Governor Bustamante personally inspected La Jicarilla in November 1723. He traveled over the mountains from Taos and visited three *rancherías* in succession, from present-day Cimarron down to the Canadian River. At every locale the Jicarilla Apaches expressed a willingness to accept a priest and his religion as well as live like the Pueblo Indians if they could receive Spanish protection. Bustamante reported this and repeated Valverde's plan to establish a presidio with fifty soldiers at La Jicarilla.

The viceroy had all but ordered compliance with Bustamente's report when Pedro de Rivera, an inspector appointed by the viceroy, wrote from New Mexico that he did not agree with the governor. Why, Rivera argued, extend Spanish civilization beyond its current limits when within the geographical bounds of that civilization there was much open land that still needed to be settled? The Jicarillas, he continued, were more concerned with defense from their Comanche enemies than with any fidelity to Spain or Catholicism. Let them move into New Mexico, perhaps around Taos. In that way Taos would be too strong for the Comanches or the French to attack.

Although Bustamante seemed to be an active as well as level-headed governor, Rivera's report caught the viceroy's attention and that of his assistant, the *fiscál*. No presidio was established. Not considered in all the rationale about moving the Jicarillas into the Taos Valley was the fact that they were a buffer and, after they moved, the enemy, whomever that might be, had a straight shot into New Mexico.

Bustamante saw his problems stemming from the Comanches, Utes, and the French. At one point in 1724, the governor led a successful chase after the Comanches. He heard tales of the French in "red coats" moving into Cuartelejo. In fact some Frenchmen did move into Cuartelejo but they soon left. When he caught up with the Comanches he rescued sixty-four Jicarillas. Bustamante never encounted Frenchmen.

The governor recommended and volunteered to lead an expedition to Cuartelejo to seek out the French, but the *fiscál* advised that the viceroy refuse permission for the proposal. France and Spain were at war when Villasur marched, but now in 1727 peace existed in Europe. Because Cuartelejo, by New Mexico's own arguments, was too far from the settlements for any French attack to be taken seriously, and because there were only traders wishing to exchange goods with the Plains Indians, not an army, the governor was told not to be overly concerned with the matter. Rivera's report was in keeping with the overall concern of Spain for New World possessions. The emphasis had shifted from expanding its empire to consolidation and economization. The system was already overburdened; increasing territory would only exacerbate the problem.

Bustamante appears to have followed his viceroy's suggestions. In 1727, the governor led a second inspection of La Jicarilla, but he gave up all attempts to establish a garrison there. Generally the French ceased to be perceived as a major threat to New Mexico, though they were still active. Étienne Veniard, Sieur de Bourgmont, acting in accordance with French policy to follow up on de Tisne's advances, traveled up the Missouri River, where he built a fort at the Wakenda tributary. He named it Fort Orleans. The next summer Bourgmont traveled to the Kansa Indians beyond the Missouri's big bend. He returned in September to travel through Kansa Indian territory and make contact with the Comanches. He left them gifts and felt that he had secured their alliance, thus opening the way to Santa Fe—not for conquest, but trade. But Bourgmont's satisfaction was premature.

The Comanches were ironically armed with French guns, and dangerous. They understood the importance of these new weapons and they did everything possible to keep them out of the hands of their enemies. As a result, the Comanches refused to permit the French to pass through their territory to get to the next tribe.

Thus, for eleven years after Rivera's report, the French were stymied in their efforts to reach New Mexico. In 1739 a French party finally got through the Comanche barrier. Brothers Pierre and Paul Mallet and seven others completed the first known French venture to Santa Fe. They began their journey in the Illinois country, where Villasur was ambushed nineteen years earlier, and traveled up the Missouri River to the Platte River. From that point Indians guided them southwest to the Arkansas River, where they found Spanish inscriptions on rocks. They traveled into New Mexico, where they arrived at Picurís Pueblo.

The French party was treated well. After several months sojourn they were allowed to leave from Pecos Pueblo. Two men stayed in New Mexico while the seven others left. They traveled down the Canadian River for ten days until they came upon a Comanche village near the present Texas-Oklahoma border. The party split up, with three of the men returning to the Illinois country and the remaining four going to New Orleans. Those going to New Orleans took with them a letter from the vicar in Santa Fe, Father Santiago de Roybal, to a priest in New Orleans. The New Mexican requested supplies, thus giving the appearance of foreign trade being allowed. The letter and the nice reception given the Mallet party stimulated interest in Santa Fe. Not surprisingly, the Mallets returned in 1741.

For the next eleven years Frenchmen started arriving on an almost annual basis, especially if we assume that many more men than those reported were involved in the illicit trade. The royal government in Mexico City and Madrid saw New Mexico and the rest of the northern frontier of New Spain as a bulwark to protect the interior provinces from foreign invasion. But New Mexicans did not see the French as any kind of pressing danger. The influx of Europeans and their trade goods were welcomed, no matter how miniscule the numbers. They were especially appreciated if they had a useful talent. In 1749, for example, the local laws against foreigners were relaxed when two Frenchmen and an Englishman came into a Taos trade fair with some Plains Indians. They had come across the plains with a party of thirty-three men. After coming upon a Jicarilla village, the three men convinced the Indians and their colleagues to allow them to go along with the Indians to New Mexico. On arriving they were gladly accepted because two of them were carpenters and the third was a tailor, barber, and bloodletter.

In 1750, a group of seven Frenchmen arrived in Santa Fe and reported Indian wars on the plains. They described incidents of cannibalism among the Indians and fierce fighting. Information such as this was solicited by the officials in New Mexico, for their big problem with the plains was not Frenchmen but Comanches.

Nevertheless, the Spanish crown was determined to put a stop to France's perceived expansive desires and in 1751 New Mexico received a royal order forbidding the government from allowing foreigners to return. Instead they were to be arrested. A pattern of French travel across the plains had started to develop, but France's real goal was to open trade. Some talk of taking over the area could be heard, but like Peñalosa, that was not taken seriously. Then there was the official entry of two Frenchmen who carried documents from their commander at Fort Chartres in Illinois. They were "to make the discovery of New Mexico" and to take goods for trade. An inventory of their merchandise includes a predominance of cloth. Bolts of coarse wool, lace, and silk prevailed. A bolt of calico anticipated its later popularity in the Rocky Mountain region. In accordance with the new policy the two men were arrested and eventually sent to Spain. Their goods were confiscated.

Meanwhile, New Mexico's people seemed to have lost some interest in the plains. By 1740 the Comanches had become a foe so formidable that they were bringing death and destruction to the small colony almost at will. The Straits of Anian obviously had not been found toward the northeast. With the increasing interest in and subsequent settlement of California, attention for exploration turned to the west and northwest of landlocked New Mexico. A map that dates from 1740 to 1756, based on the information and drawings of Santa Fe cartographer Bernardo Miera y Pacheco shows a large, white, mythical city on the banks of an equally mythical great river that is flowing toward California. Both city and river are located to the northwest of New Mexico. The one grand exploratory expedition, led by two Franciscans, went northwest out of New Mexico in 1776 to find a trade route to Monterey, California. That expedition partially followed the route of an earlier, less documented trip. A few years later Juan Bautista de Anza, a future governor of New Mexico, tried to establish a trade route to New Mexico from Sonora, southwest of the secluded colony.

By 1740 the Comanches had pushed the Apaches into New Mexico, and the Spanish and Pueblo settlements of New Mexico became the recipients of fierce raids. New Mexico was a natural attraction to the nomadic Comanches. Horses, blankets, and food, especially at harvest time, brought the Comanches as well as other marauding Indians to New Mexico. Plains Indians had long traveled to New Mexico to trade or raid the settlements.

Now the Plains Indians were armed and mounted while the Pueblo Indians were only mounted. Spanish antipathy to giving weapons to Indians did not help in the defense of the Pueblos who shared the same enemies.

Another custom both helped the adversaries and gave rise to more antagonism. The trade fairs brought people together, usually at Taos, sometimes at Pecos or, later, in Abiquiu. Plains Indians like the Comanches brought in hides, meat, salt, suet to make tallow, and prisoners to trade for blankets, pottery, maize, stones (usually turquoise), and prisoners. The exchange of prisoners gave rise to slave raiding on both sides and, naturally, there was a high incidence of Indian raiding around the time of the trade fairs. The last was a matter of convenience because of the trade fairs' proximity to the settlements.

As the raids continued, New Mexico became less able to cope with the enemy Indians. The province was poor. Even some of the presidial troops lacked firearms. The soldiers are described as mostly having lances and bows and arrows. These men became very adept in the use of the lance, a trait that continued into the nineteenth century. The lance also gave rise to a plains hazard. One of New Mexico's casualties was caused when a soldier was riding on patrol out on the plains. He was holding his lance upright, no doubt resting it on his foot or stirrup, when a bolt of lightning struck the lance and killed the him.

In 1749 Tomás Vélez Cachupín began the first of two remarkable terms as governor of New Mexico. Vélez was one of those men who stood out with his Indian policies, which anticipated the success of Juan Bautista de Anza who ultimately would solve the Comanche problem.

Vélez sought to make peace through trade. At the first opportunity he traveled up to the Taos trade fair where the Comanches had set up a camp of forty tepees. He offered gifts and peace to the Comanches but warned that if they did not keep the agreement he would declare war. Surprisingly, the tactic initially worked for four months.

Then in early November a band of three hundred Comanches raided Pecos and Galisteo. The Comanches had no reason to take the Spanish seriously. None of the governors or their men had presented a military threat in the past. The Comanches traditionally had been cheated at the trade fairs and they had no reason but to carry on as usual.

Governor Vélez was not usual and upon hearing of the violation of the truce he gathered fifty-four soldiers, thirty citizens, and a number of Pueblo

DEDI_ADO
AL S.T F. LIPE CAVA
LLERO DE BA   ONEL DE LOS REA
LES EXERCITOS D   1. PRIMÈR AYUDAN
TE MAYÒR DEL R   MIENTO DE SUS REA
LES GUARDIAS ESPAÑOLAS DE YNFANTE
RIA, SECRETARIO DE CAMARA Y DEL
VIRREYNATO DE LAS PROVINCIAS
DE NUEVA ESPAÑA.

BERNARDO MIERA Y PACHECO MAP, 1740-56

Collection of the Palace of the Governors, Santa Fe, New Mexico.

Confluence of the Platte and Loup rivers where the Villasur expedition was ambushed in 1720 by Indians allied with the French.

Indians and followed the Comanche raiders out onto the plains. On the fourth day the trail divided, one branch heading to the northeast and the other trail going southeast. Veléz chose the southern route. He kept scouts out three leagues, almost eight miles ahead of the contingent which "cautiously marched day and night" in freezing temperatures. The governor only permitted stops of two or three hours to pasture the horses and give the soldiers a short rest.

True to his intuition, the Comanches were surprised at a water hole. Through a night of fighting, during which Veléz ordered bonfires built to light the field, the enemy backed into the water to take refuge in the reeds and thicket. Veléz ordered a ceasefire around midnight when all but a few of the Comanches surrendered.

Fighting resumed when the holdouts attempted to break through the seige. They were repulsed, and the last of the survivors surrendered. Veléz writes, "When daylight...came, the water hole and its environs were seen to be covered with dead bodies."

Veléz's subsequent kind treatment and release of the Comanche survivors, especially after the success of his pursuit, won a lasting peace for the remainder of his first administration and all of his second administration. Only during a eight-year hiatus between his two terms did war break out again. Within the first year after the end of his first term, the Comanches devastated Taos Pueblo, killing most of the men and capturing fifty women. The next year an expedition was claimed to have resulted in the deaths of four hundred Comanches after chasing them onto the plains. This outbreak of hostilities occurred because of the incompetence of the three governors who replaced Veléz but did not continue his policies.

Veléz's policy extended beyond gifts, promises, and punishment. He understood that the Comanches had reason to war upon New Mexico and so he personally attended the trade fairs to prevent cheating. He also used his own troops to guard the Comanches' horses to prevent theft. He prevailed upon the Carlana, Cuartelejo, and Paloma Apaches to accept his protection against the Comanches. He kept two hundred men at Santa Fe ready to march within a day and worked with the settlers to improve his militia. To avoid surprises he dispatched spies who roamed as far as the Canadian River.

Pedro Fermín de Mendinueta took Veléz's place in 1768 and, just like at the end of the latter's first term, fighting broke out immediately. Perhaps the Comanches felt they had an agreement with the man and not the government. More likely Veléz's successors did not agree with his policies, although a combination of both reasons is probably closer to the truth. Two campaigns against the Comanches were mounted after Mendinueta's first year in office. The second campaign, with a total of 546 men, including presidials, militia, Pueblos, Utes, and Apaches, traveled northeast to the Arkansas River. Neither effort achieved any success. To the contrary, Mendinueta's policy of war resulted in the disintegration of Comanche relations that would not be restored for two decades, under Governor Juan Bautista de Anza.

In October 1768 the Comanches entered the Río Grande Valley, led by a chief "who wore a device, a green horn on his forehead, fixed in a headdress or on a tanned leather headpiece." This person, called Green Horn, "Cuerno Verde," would become legendary and seemingly invincible.

Cuerno Verde and his people raided with impunity. No village in New Mexico was safe. The raids came from the Plains and, sometimes, from the north down the Chama River Valley. Mendinueta, learning firsthand about Veléz's warnings, sent out punitive expeditions. The largest and most successful involved six hundred men who traveled one hundred and twenty miles before engaging the Comanches, killing two hundred and fifty out of four hundred of the enemy.

Despite these momentary successes, Mendinueta had to agree with Veléz's earlier assessment that New Mexico could be in peril over a prolonged period of warfare. New Mexico was slowly being defeated. The population was dwindling and the people becoming more desperate. Part of the problem was official unconcern. As far as anyone could see, New Mexico had no natural wealth, and its agricultural economy had no value to anyone but New Mexicans. The province had never been a moneymaker. Mendinueta wrote that the problem of survival had deteriorated by 1775 to the point that the viceroy should send horses rather than guns. Most of the horses in New Mexico had been stolen.

By 1776, the Spanish government was undergoing a number of reforms under the leadership of the Bourbon King, Carlos III. More attention was being paid to New Mexico. France had secretly ceded Louisiana to Spain prior to the end of the Seven Years War in 1763. This aquisition resulted in some policy changes, for now both "shores" of the plains belonged to Spain.

New Mexico was included in an administrative reorganization that created a captain-generalship of Interior Provinces, which were to be separated from the viceroyalty of New Spain. The interior provinces were

Juan Bautista de Anza from an original oil painting attributed to
Fray Orci in Mexico City, 1774.

placed under a military government independent from the viceroy in Mexico City.

While some of the resources for these reforms were diverted to Spain's effort in fighting Britain during the war for United States independence, New Mexico did benefit from the appointment of Juan Bautista de Anza as governor of New Mexico in 1777. Anza brought with him to New Mexico the same attitude that Veléz had. In addition, he had the interest of Spanish officialdom. One of his major goals was to win over the Comanches so that the rest of the frontier could concentrate on subduing hostile Apaches who had become a major menace in Texas, Chihuahua, Sonora, and Arizona. Perhaps Anza could even use the Comanches as allies against the Apaches.

Along with successfully defeating the Hopis and breaking a Navajo-Gila Apache alliance to the west of the Río Grande, Anza won over the Utes and then concentrated on the Comanches. Recognizing that Cuerno Verde had an unbending hatred for the Spanish, Anza gathered a force and went after the legendary Comanche. Using the tactic of taking an indirect route to the Comanche home territory on the Arkansas River, the governor was able to surprise the Comanches and win a major victory in the initial battle. However, Anza did not succeed in capturing or killing Cuerno Verde, so he continued his pursuit. This resulted in a day-long battle near Greenhorn Peak, Colorado. The New Mexicans defeated the Comanches again, this time killing Cuerno Verde, his oldest son, and many other Comanche leaders. This defeat won a peace that lasted at least a generation.

With the last great Indian barrier removed from the northeast, a new threat ensued. "Los Americanos," those people from the United States, shared the same desire their predecessors from the other side of the plains had. Horses and mules replaced the mythical silver mines as the goal for trade with New Mexico. Spanish policy reacted to the new nation by trying to create Indian resistance to its expansion. To encourage this resistance, Spanish policy changed enough to allow the giving of guns to some of the tribes, including the now-friendly Comanches. In keeping with this new policy and the recently won peace, a new avenue of trade and commerce opened up for New Mexico. The peace allowed many New Mexicans to draw on their experience and background to fan out over the plains to hunt and trade. The hunters, called *ciboleros*, developed a commerce in buffalo hides. *Comancheros* traded on the plains and acquired their name because they mostly traded and lived among the Comanches, thus cementing a lasting relationship.

Spanish officialdom figured that the peace provided an opportunity to open up trade and communications between New Mexico and St. Louis in the Province of Louisiana. In Santa Fe at the time was Pedro Vial, a Frenchman from New Orleans who, like l'Archevêque before him, became a Spanish citizen and moved to New Mexico. Governor Fernando de la Concha decided that Vial would be the proper person to lead a trip to St. Louis. Vial had extensive frontier experience. He had traveled to Santa Fe from Bexar, Texas, and then to Natchitoches and San Antonio and back.

In 1782 The Governor issued instructions to Vial and two men to begin the trip. The three traveled through Pecos Pueblo, down the Canadian River into Texas, turned northeast, and were captured by the Indians. As fortune would have it, their captors took them in the direction they had intended to travel, for they were released on the Republican River. In the company of some traders from St. Louis, they completed their trip floating down the Republican and Missouri Rivers.

The return trip followed the same route and had less adventure. The party traveled up the Missouri River into the Pawnee country by boat, again accompanied by St. Louis traders. (The fact that in both directions they were accompanied by men from St. Louis indicates the extent and distance of trade being initiated from the eastern end of the trail.) The trip to St. Louis took 136 days, the return journey twenty days longer.

NEWCOMERS AT THE GATE

In 1800 Spain ceded Louisiana territory back to France, and New Mexico once again became a borderland. But if the career of Juan Lucero is any indication, around the turn of the century plains travel for New Mexicans had become routine. Lucero made thirteen known trips between 1788 and 1819, as far east as the Texas panhandle and the Arkansas River in Kansas and Colorado, and as far north as present day Colorado Springs.

When the United States acquired Louisiana from France in 1803, the purchase rekindled a fascination with New Mexico among people in the Mississippi Valley. American traders started illegally entering New Mexico's domain to trade. They were usually met on the plains by New Mexican hunters and traders who gave them directions while sending word back to the settlements. In 1805 many Americans, most with French surnames, arrived in Santa Fe. the following year Zebulon Montgomery Pike led an expedition from St. Louis to the Arkansas River and over La Veta Pass, arriving in January 1807 in the San Luis Valley where New Mexican soldiers detained the party for trespassing.

Like Pike and his men, not every United States citizen, French surnamed or not, was welcomed. In 1805 and 1806 Governor Joaquin del Real Alencaster sent Pedro Vial on two expeditions that for various reasons did not pass beyond the Arkansas River. The governor then commissioned the newly arrived Facundo Melgares to reconnoiter the plains in search of foreigners attempting to reach New Mexico from the United States. Melgares took one hundred and five soldiers, four hundred militiamen, and one hundred Indians with enough provisions for six months. He went down the Canadian River and then proceeded northward into the lands of the Pawnees, where he handed out some Spanish medals that are now considered sacred by the Southern Pawnees. The expedition traveled as far as the Republican River in

Peace Medal (two views), 1797. Found among the northern Pawnee Indians and traded from New Mexico between 1800 and 1820.
Courtesy of Nebraska State Historical Society, A.T. Hill Collection.

southern Nebraska and may have entered Missouri. They reported no evidence of foreigners, having missed Pike's expedition by a month.

Despite the risks, Americans continued to venture to New Mexico. Some, like Robert McKnight and two partners, had the misfortune of bad timing, for they arrived in New Mexico in 1812, just in time to be connected with the attempted flight of a Mexican revolutionary leader, Father Miguel Hidalgo y Costilla, to the United States. McKnight and his friends were arrested as conspirators in the planned Hidalgo escape and spent eight years in jail.

By that time, American merchants were no longer a novelty in Santa Fe. The path across the vast, inland ocean of the Great Plains had become well worn by Indians, Spaniards, Frenchman, and Americans. During the good months the plains were well peopled with traders, hunters, and Spanish military parties.

By 1810, United States merchants were no longer a novelty in Santa Fe. The path across the vastness of the inland ocean known as the plains had become well worn by Indians, Spaniards, Frenchmen, and North Americans. During the good months the plains were well peopled with traders, hunters, and Spanish military parties. As one anonymous report in poor French noted around 1817, the governor sent patrols "to reconnoiter the country and see what is going on there." The last of the major Spanish expeditions set out in 1818 to search the Yellowstone River area to learn of any foreign plans. The expedition returned to report of a rivalry between Britain and the United States in the area and that two British forts had been constructed.

In 1821, when Mexico achieved its independence from Spain, the old Spanish closed-border, mercantilist system gave way to a new open-border system inviting foreign commerce. William Becknell was one of many people to traverse what would become the Santa Fe Trail. He was even met on the plains by a New Mexican patrol that escorted his party into Santa Fe. However, Becknell's party was the first to arrive after Mexican Independence; by fate, to him goes the credit of opening the Santa Fe Trail.

Nevertheless, Becknell's trail was a route over which many people and much commerce already had traveled. While early historians of the plains and the Santa Fe Trail like to claim those two subjects within the context of United States history, many times at the expense of Spaniards, the way was prepared by other sons of Europe who were not intimidated by the vastness of the area. They did not settle on the plains, but neither did any other Europeans or their New World descendants until the last third of the nineteenth century.

By the time the Santa Fe Trail opened in 1821, there was not a place on the plains that had not been explored by Spaniards. That exploration had not been accomplished easily or quickly. The stories of hardship, bravery, determination, suffering, and success predating 1821 are every bit as exciting, even romantic, as those that followed. Historians will have to learn to delve into the accounts of these earlier people who wrote in Spanish or French—or not at all. And, as this earlier, more amazing story of almost three centuries surfaces, the heritage of the United States will be enriched. The Santa Fe Trail, that corridor across the plains from New Mexico to eastern Kansas and Missouri, is yet another stitch on the multicolored tapestry of American history. Perhaps historians will understand the role that the descendants of Spain and Mexico played in the subsequent history of the Santa Fe Trail and the transcontinental development of the United States. Columbus's legacy was not just a sea voyage but an attitude that eventually garnered the geographical knowledge of the whole interior of the North American continent. New Mexico was the island from which most of that exploration took place.

Appendix: Maps

1540-1541

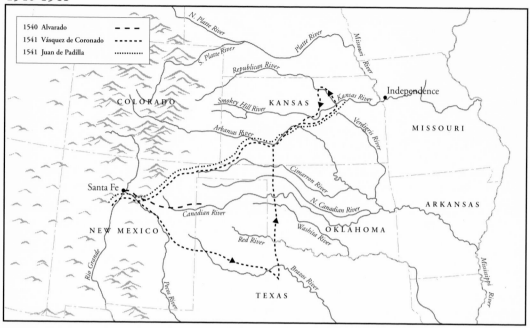

Legend:
- 1540 Alvarado — — —
- 1541 Vásquez de Coronado – – –
- 1541 Juan de Padilla ....

1581-1593

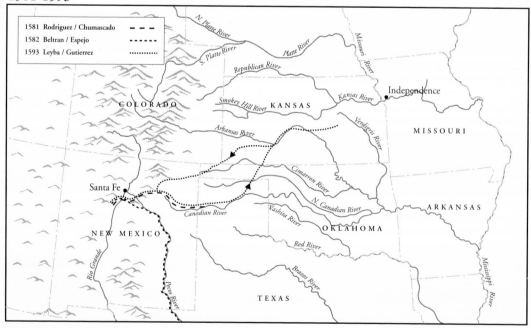

Legend:
- 1581 Rodriguez / Chumascado — — —
- 1582 Beltran / Espejo – – –
- 1593 Leyba / Gutierrez ....

1598-1665

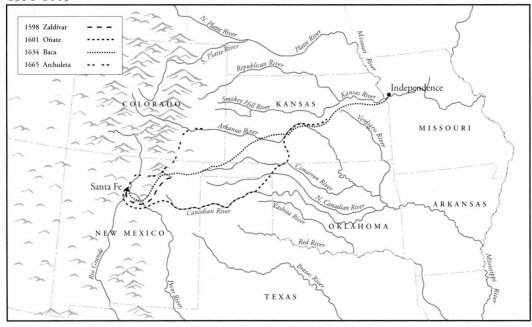

1598	Zaldívar	– – –
1601	Oñate	- - - -
1634	Baca	············
1665	Archuleta	– ·· –

1696-1714

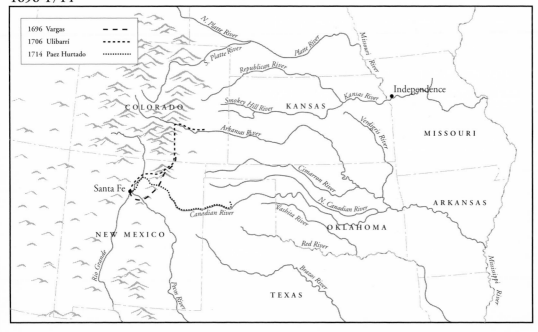

1696	Vargas	– – –
1706	Ulibarrí	- - - -
1714	Paez Hurtado	············

1719-1751

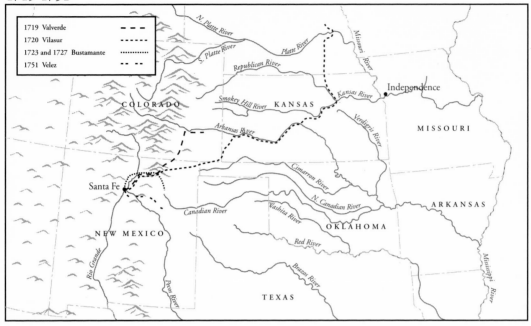

1768-1782

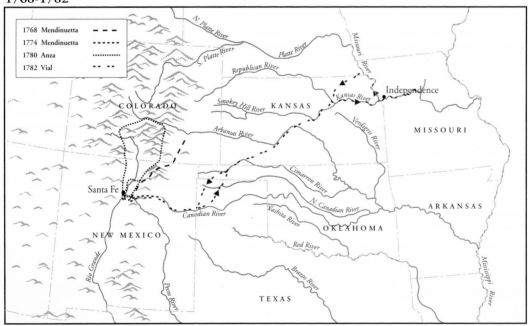

1805-1810

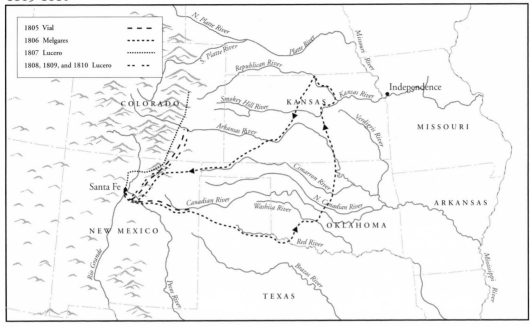

Legend:
1805 Vial	– – –
1806 Melgares	- - -
1807 Lucero	·········
1808, 1809, and 1810 Lucero	–– ––

1821-1880

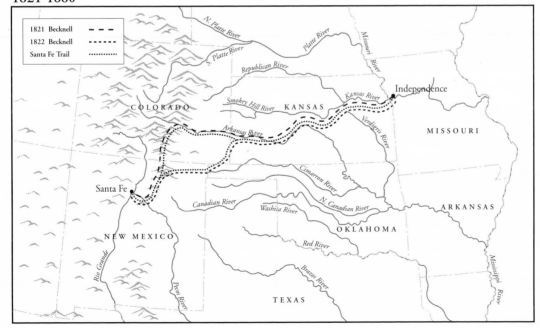

Legend:
1821 Becknell	–– ––
1822 Becknell	- - -
Santa Fe Trail	·········

Maps by Magellan Geographix, Santa Barbara, California

SUGGESTED READING

John Francis Bannon. *The Spanish Borderlands Frontier*. New York: Holt, Rinehart, & Winston, 1970.

William Brandon. *Quivira: Europeans in the Region of the Santa Fe Trail, 1540-1820*. Athens, Ohio: University Press, 1990.

George P. Hammond & Agapito Rey. *The Rediscovery of New Mexico, 1580-1594*. Albuquerque: University of New Mexico Press, 1966.

George P. Hammond & Agapito Rey. *Don Juan de Oñate: Colonizer of New Mexico, 1595-1628*. Albuquerque: University of New Mexico Press, 1953.

George P. Hammond & Agapito Rey. *Narratives of the Coronado Expedition, 1540-1542*. Albuquerque: University of New Mexico Press, 1940.

Gottfried Hotz. *The Segesser Paintings: Masterpieces Depicting Spanish Colonial New Mexico*. Santa Fe: Museum of New Mexico Press, 1991.

Noel M. Loomis & Abraham P. Nasatir. *Pedro Vial and the Roads to Santa Fe*. Norman: University of Oklahoma Press, 1967.

Abraham P. Nasatir. *Borderlands in Retreat: From Spanish Louisiana to the Far Southwest*. Albuquerque: University of New Mexico Press, 1976.

Marc Simmons. *The Last Conquistador: Juan de Oñate and the Settling of the Far Southwest*. Norman: University of Oklahoma, 1991.

Alfred B. Thomas. *The Plains Indians and New Mexico, 1751-1778: A Collection of Documents Illustrative of the History of the Eastern Frontier of New Mexico*. Albuquerque: University of New Mexico Press, 1940.

Alfred B. Thomas. *After Coronado: Spanish Exploration Northeast of New Mexico, 1696-1727*. Norman: University of Oklahoma Press, 1935.

Alfred B. Thomas. *Forgotten Frontiers: A Study of the Spanish Indian Policy of Don Juan Bautista de Anza, Governor of New Mexico, 1777-1787*. Norman: University of Oklahoma Press, 1932.